Touched by a Hummingbird

Written & Illustrated By Norma K. Salway

JWB
Just Write Books

The story of how an encounter with a hummingbird touched the heart of one mourning a loss of a friend.

In Memory of
Nancy Bailey Young

© 2011 Norma K. Salway All Rights Reserved.
All illustrations by Norma K. Salway
ISBN: 978-1-934949-46-7
Printed in the USA
Just Write Books, Topsham, Maine www.jstwrite.com

My heart was heavy with grief that August morning. A special friend had just died. She was a cherished person known to all in our small Maine community.

As I stood by the kitchen sink gazing out the window, I suddenly heard a faint thumping sound from the nearby garage.

I opened the screen door and stepped
down into the garage. My eyes spanned
the corners, searching for the source of
the noise. Humid warm air filled the wide
open area.
Soon, I spied the source of the sound—
a female ruby-throated hummingbird.
She was frantically fluttering her wings
against the side of an upper windowpane,
trying to escape the spiral threads of a spider's web.
As I watched, she unexpectedly freed
herself and flew to the far side of the
garage to another light-filled window.
But, once her tiny wings touched the glass,
she again traversed the garage searching
for a means of escape.

Quickly, I reached into the corner of the garage for a long-handled broom, hoping to gently guide the stranded hummingbird to the freedom of the front yard.

Instead, valiantly, she escaped to the top of the panels of the old raised-panel wooden garage door. There she sat, momentarily resting her lacy wings. She hovered before once again flitting from window to window in vain.

Swiftly, I raced to the nearby
perennial garden to pluck a tall
wilting flower. I hoped to attract
the frantic bird to the aroma of nectar.
I've learned since that hummingbirds
have no sense of smell. However,
upon my return, there was no sign of her.

I peered into every corner, every window, even the tops of hanging garden tools and along the raised door panel.
Nothing.
"She must have safely flown through the open doorway," I whispered to myself, relieved at the thought that she had escaped the confines of the stifling garage.

A while later, I was preparing for a trip into town to run errands. As I backed the car out of the garage, I pressed the button to automatically close the door. I took one last look around. I wiped my forehead. We were in the middle of a heat wave with daytime temperatures rising into the nineties.

An hour later, I returned. After making several trips to and from the car, I lowered the aged door.

I sat down at the kitchen table to eat my lunch under the refreshing breeze of the overhead ceiling fan.

*Later, as the temperature continued to rise,
I ventured outside to check on the condition
of my pumpkin patch. As I reentered the garage,
I suddenly noticed the hummingbird!*

*There she was, almost under the rear of my car,
barely able to sit upright on the hot concrete floor.
Steaming rays of sunshine poured down upon her.
Shaking slightly, eyes nearly closed, she never
moved as I walked closer.*

*"You poor thing. You've been in this hot garage
the whole time. You must be thirsty!" I uttered aloud,
as I knelt down to get a closer look.*

*Hastily, I reached for the stalks of flowers
I'd attempted to use earlier in the day. Carefully,
I slipped the thick stalks of fading yellow flowers
under the limp body and scooped her up.
Hugging the stalks, I carried the quivering patient
to the shade of the covered patio
and pots of flowering plants.
My mind was racing with plans for action as I
placed the bird-laden stalks across a pot of pink-
hued blossoms. Nectar! Water!
She needed nourishment!*

*Slowly I tipped the stalks so the bill of the tiny creature was tilting down inside one of the tubular blossoms.
In the meantime, I rushed into the kitchen for a cup of water, hoping somehow to get her hydrated.*

I realized that the water should be boiled and cooled first, but there just wasn't time.

Upon returning with the cup of water, I again tipped the plant stalks and patient, enabling the hummingbird's long tapered bill to reach down into the cup of clear water.
As soon as the water touched the tip of her bill, the hummingbird's long tongue emerged to sip. After this first drink, she lifted her head to swallow. Again and again, I tipped the stalks, directing her bill each time down into the cup.
Each time, she sipped, tipped her head upward and swallowed.

*For several minutes, I continued to hydrate
the tiny patient. Soon, her little body
stopped shivering. However, she still
appeared unable to move.
Then I realized that in my haste to deliver
water to the seemingly overheated bird,
I had neglected to add sugar.
Once again I dashed into the house.
This time, I pinched a bit of sugar from
the sugar bowl and stirred it
into the cup of water.
On my return trip back outside,
I snatched my camera.
"I'll never be this close to a hummingbird again,"
I thought.*

*However, this time, when I attempted to
tip the hummingbird's beak into the cup,
she declined to drink.
Determined, I stuck my index finger
into the sugar-water and withdrew
a droplet that stuck to the tip of my finger.
I placed the droplet directly over the
little feathered head and let the water s-l-o-w-l-y
slip off.
As soon as the drop of sugar-water touched her bill,
she eagerly began to drink and drink.
I continued to dunk my finger, place the droplet
over her beak, and release the drops
over and over again.
I watched with amazement as she willingly
accepted nourishment from me.*

As the hummingbird drank each additional sip, I was moved by the experience—overwhelmed with the wonder and beauty of this miraculous tiny creature as she allowed me to hand feed her. After she stopped sipping, I reached for my camera. As I leaned over to get a closer angle, she attempted to ruffle her feathers.
I noticed, then, that her eyes appeared to have something covering them.
Looking closer, I realized that gossamer cobwebs had become snagged in her feathers and buttoned shut one of her round black eyes.

*Again, I returned to the kitchen, this time
to retrieve a pair of small manicure scissors.
Picking up a short piece of plant stem, I used
it to carefully pull away a thin strand of the web.
A piece of a spider's web was entangled at the
edge of a tiny feather about a quarter of an inch
from the hummingbird's eye.
Carefully, I snipped the white stretchy thread.
To my surprise, a little round eye popped opened.
"Yeah! I cried softly to her. Just look at you!"*

As I examined the hummingbird more closely,
I found more of the strong white cobweb
snarled in her wings and wrapped
around her tiny feet. She must have fallen
victim to the strong silken threads of a
spider's web earlier in the morning.
I felt like a surgeon as I cut away several
strands of the web. I was amazed at the elasticity
and strength of each strand. With each snip, I
became more aware of how tangled the
hummingbird had become.
No wonder she was unable to fly.
The last fragment of spider's web
remained wrapped around both a foot
and a wing of the hummingbird.

*Slowly, I raised and pulled the strand very slightly.
Carefully, I made a final snip.
To my astonishment, the hummingbird suddenly
flapped her newly-freed wings and alertly
flew to the nearby crabapple tree!
As she flew against the hazy blue sky,
I heard her chirp softly.
Never in my life had I heard a song
from a hummingbird, only the hum
of its wings.
"Good-bye," I called to her.*

The next morning, I attended the funeral honoring my departed friend. Placed on the seat of each chair was a small white card listing the order of the service. There on the front cover of the commemorative program was the image of a ruby-throated hummingbird sipping nectar from a flower.

After my experience, I learned that hummingbirds are actually able to enter into a slowed state of metabolism called torpor. During torpor, fluids are reabsorbed by the kidneys to help prevent dehydration. This state is unique to hummingbirds.

Did you know?

Hummingbirds use threads of spider webs to secure their nests to branches.

During torpor, feathers are fluffed out, eyes are closed, and the birds often shiver.

Hummingbirds have the smallest eggs in the world.

Hummingbirds are the smallest birds in the world.

Known for eating insects, spiders, flowers, nectar, and sap, hummingbirds are omnivores.

Hummingbirds fly forwards, backwards, at eighty wing beats per second.

A group of hummingbirds is called a "charm."

Resources: BirdWatching-Bliss.com, EnchantedLearning.com, MostAmazingNews.com

CPSIA information can be obtained
at www.ICGtesting.com
Printed in the USA
LVIW011320030812
292818LV00001B